Summons

Summons

◆◆◆◆◆◆◆ POEMS ◆◆◆◆◆◆◆◆◆◆◆◆◆
Deborah Tall

Winner of the 1999
Kathryn A. Morton Prize in Poetry
Selected by Charles Simic

Sarabande Books
LOUISVILLE, KENTUCKY

Managing Editor
Sarabande Books, Inc.
2234 Dundee Road, Suite 200
Louisville, KY 40205

LIBRARY OF CONGRESS CATALOGING-IN-PUBLICATION DATA

Tall, Deborah
    Summons : poems / by Deborah Tall ; selected by Charles Simic.
        p.   cm.
    "Winner of the 1999 Kathryn A. Morton Prize in Poetry."
    ISBN 1-889330-49-3 (cloth: alk. paper) — ISBN 1-889330-50-7 (pbk:
    alk. paper)
        I. Simic, Charles, 1938– II. Title.

PS3570.A397 S8 2000
811'.54—dc21   00-021255

Cover painting: *Dunmore Head Interior,* by Barbara Kassel. Provided courtesy of the artist.

Cover and text design by Charles Casey Martin.

Manufactured in the United States of America.
This book is printed on acid-free paper.

Sarabande Books is a nonprofit literary organization.

Special thanks to Anonymous (3), Anne Axton, Linda Bruckheimer, The Louise and Ardè Bulova Fund, William and Gail Gorham, Susan Griffin and Douglas Sharps, Richard Howorth, John Jacob, Nana Lampton, Roland and Eleanor Miller, Stephen Reily and Emily Bingham, Peter Saunders, Judith Slater, Dan Sully, and The Sunshine Fund/New York Community Trust.

to the memory of
Toni Flores

She'll come when called.
Her high chiming is hourless.

Acknowledgments

Much gratitude to those who helped these poems become themselves: Rosanna Warren, Stephen Kuusisto, Susan Holahan, Eavan Boland, and especially David Weiss.

Thanks to the MacDowell Colony, Yaddo, and the Ingram Merrill Foundation for providing time during which a number of these poems were written.

And thanks as well to the editors of the following magazines, where many of these poems first appeared (sometimes in different versions).

Agni: "We'll Never Change Our Tune"

Antaeus: "Remains"

Colorado Review: "Constellated," "Search"

Controlled Burn: "Spirit"

Epoch: "Dividing of Ways," Wood Song"

Fence: "Commitment"

The Georgia Review: "Prayer"

The Gettysburg Review: "Heat," "Landscape," "The Last Horseman," "Marching Orders"

The Nation: "The Balloons," "Gesture" (under the title "Sign"), "The Rule of Berries"

Partisan Review: "Bog," "Children's Beach Museum"

Ploughshares: "Cleaning Smelt," "Daybreak," "The Miraculous Mandarin"

Poetry: "Grounded"

Prairie Schooner: "Whereof Are You Made"

Williwaw: "Myrrha"

"Prayer" and "Gesture" (as "Sign") were reprinted in *The Anthology of American Verse and Yearbook of American Poetry* (editions of 1988 and 1989).

"Cleaning Smelt" was reprinted in *The State Street Reader* (1990).

"Landscape" was reprinted in *Writing Poems* (Longman, 2000).

An excerpt from "Daybreak" was included in the Poetry Desk Calendar for 2000.

Several of these poems also appeared in a chapbook, *Come Wind, Come Weather*, published by State Street Press.

Table of Contents

Foreword

There are a number of ways in which a poet may captivate the reader: It could be that the unusual subject matter of the poems is appealing; or it could be that the imagination of the poet is overflowing with unexpected and delightful analogies; or it could be the voice of the poet, so intimate, the reader feels individually spoken to; or it could be, finally, the poet's ear, so sensitive to nuances of sound and connotations of words, it is as if one is hearing the language one uses daily, in all its meaning and beauty, for the very first time.

Reading Deborah Tall's collection *Summons*, I was reminded of these truths. On the one hand, hers is a book of mostly short poems, poems about small events vividly recollected, and on the other hand, every one of her poems is a huge feast of words and images. Tall's strategy, like Emily Dickinson's, is to isolate a word or phrase, pare it down even further, and then mull it over until all its richness of meaning becomes apparent. Attention and care for detail for both of them are a form of devotion, a moral stance. Particulars matter. Compassion for creatures big and small, with which Deborah Tall's poems are filled, is an integral part of her technique. A true artist is serious about the way she employs her craft.

The art of prosody, of which Deborah Tall is a master, is a jeweler's art. It is about ascertaining the weight of words, measuring each one of them in turn against silence and time. Here, for instance, is how her poem "Eternity in Days" begins:

One last lick of daylight
lids the lake. Smoke
thins

Simple words made extraordinary by the deliberateness of their arrangement. At the end of each line of the stanza, there is a pause and a brief suspense as to what comes next. The poem sets its own clock. Even before we get to the next stanza, we have learned at what speed we must proceed. Read, the poem is instructing us, so that you savor each word, so that you both hear it and see the world it points to. As we read, line by line, sounds turn into music, words and images grow in meaning. If you believe that this is what *all* poets do anyway, you are wrong. Only the best of them know how to make us reread with increasing pleasure a few lines of poetry.

Then, there are her images:

A book left open
to page 85
with bread crumbs in it.

Or:

a man at the door, rapping,
barked at, the screen door latched
against curious children.

There are many such carefully observed moments in her book in which something commonplace, something that was there all along, comes into view. The invisible made visible.

Yes, we say to ourselves, what poetry does best is to recover the immediacy and the sensation of life. We like such images because they remind us to open our eyes ourselves to where we are. The world is amazing providing we have eyes to notice what is already before our eyes.

But there's more! Deborah Tall's poems are also full of inspired flights of the imagination—visionary images that take us to another, heightened realm. The poet, as it were, gives us a broom to ride. We are up there somewhere in the sky watching:

> The night taking names
> in its notebook of stars.

Perhaps, it occurs to me, the only way to see truly how things really are is to close our eyes real tight? Because with eyes closed, we are able to feel deeply what we have just seen. Like when Deborah Tall speaks in another poem of "nightfall tightening its leash," how absolutely right that seems! I have never heard it said before, and yet now that I have, it sounds inevitable to me and true.

> Look, our house is airy, plain,
> temple to small companion things

These lines from Deborah Tall's poem "Bouquet" may be the best description of what happens in her poems. The poem is an enclosure with an altar (the white page); words, which represent "small companion things," are laid on it. The reader is a stranger who has entered the temple and now approaches the altar trying to understand what kind of gods these are. Even if poetry is not your religion, you will know soon enough that authentic divinities are to be found in these poems.

—*Charles Simic*

Summons

DIVIDING OF WAYS ◆◆◆◆◆◆◆◆◆◆◆◆◆◆◆◆

Must I admit
the birds,
unpromulgated,

the star parked
in the gable of a barn?

His horses are leaving
the house behind.

There are sets
of locks, a history
of shared lies,

a residual glow
within the several greens
called setting,

principles
heroic as a rusty bike
or shelved preserves,

a book left open
to page 85
with bread crumbs in it.

Go
set your sights
along the flight path
of all that crumbling

or lie back
until the thumb of a falling petal
imprints itself
on your very face.

HOUSEHOLD ◇◇◇◇◇◇◇◇◇◇◇◇◇◇◇◇

The way we are living,
timorous or bold,
will have been our life.

—Seamus Heaney

A man at the door, rapping,
barked at, the screen door latched
against curious children.

A man asking
for the simplest
of things—a telephone,

water.
Through the screen
I see him as if in newsprint.

Over his shoulder,
bone china, friable,
the moon in broad daylight,

silence big and lumpish
as the children's abandoned oatmeal
(silence, on which all music is written)

breathless as my heart
lying in wait
in the lifted hand of a stranger.

5

SEARCH ◆◆◆◆◆◆◆◆◆◆◆◆◆◆◆

Sara Ann Wood, missing

1.

He believes in the soul
so if coyotes (some say
they might have)
scavenged the murdered body
of his daughter

he doesn't howl
but says he'll have her back
at the resurrection

will hold her, walk with her
no bones, no heart, no weeping

2.

My fingers counting on your backbone

the spongy intersections of our bodies
    together in heat

the simultaneous kiss
    and its breaking off

when I left our baby on the gurney
for the spinal tap

howling

   3.

—fit the profile
—he was hunting
—used his knife
—used her
—remembers that she begged
   over and over

    4.

If sunlight pointed,
finger on a map

if lives came from somewhere
and found their way back

if nothing belonged to us

5.

Searching once
for a man presumed drowned:
"It takes eight days for the body
to rise. You think the body is heavy?
It's the brain holds it down.
The body? Light as a feather."

6.

Dogs and equipment
can tell where soil's
been displaced, where bodies met
and broke off.

Pattern of scatter, incision,
footfall. What
we can envision.
What we cannot get beyond.

7.

Sniffed, sifted, seen,
unseen.

Nightfall tightening its leash.

REMAINS ◆◆◆◆◆◆◆◆◆◆◆◆◆◆◆◆◆

The first rule of loss:
to cast no shadow

yet how beautiful you still were
this morning, just dead,
wingspan hugging the pavement
when I fetched you up
out of a stiff breeze
and cupped to my heart
your twin
lilac smudge-pots,
a celestial stain
on yellow wing skin
boned with black velvet

I could hardly breathe

and now, sighing too hard,
one broken wing
skids across my desk
where I have propped you
to grieve about the body
and that perilous thing
called memory (poor
substitute for soul)

"The butterfly preaches contentment"

See how I alter
you, let you
splinter to touch
symbolize
what moment to moment
I require

butterfly flower, fringe flower,
poor man's orchid—
gone like the morning mist
chaff blown from the threshing floor
smoke from a chimney

    the first rule of loss
    to cast no shadow
    though turning toward light
    was once your second nature

shreds of sky
between the blackened trees
single irises
anonymous in the gauzy dusk
grayness holding hands
with grayness
and a quick burn of silver
almost unnoticed on your dried wing tip
grazes me
like the shoulder tap
of the wandering dead

I sit quiet
invite you closer
to the single candle, starred,
the wine left uncorked

I will not flinch
even if a whole wing
should break to powder
I'd gather you back
       (*we are as water*
       thrown upon the earth
       which cannot be gathered up
       again)
I'd reconstruct you

I cannot
let you go
the way of color at dusk

I wrap you
press you into the world of objects

where you cannot heal me.

SPIRIT ◇◇◇◇◇◇◇◇◇◇◇◇◇◇◇◇

Unlike us, lives
only where she'll thrive
(would banish right angles)

burns a hole in the ceiling,
floodlights me flat
on my back

and an open window left flapping.
Wherever she goes
the taste of my tongue in my mouth.

And what the wind undoes—her hair,
the battening down, what tea leaves
tell: *Go and catch a falling star, get with child….*

It is January.
The trees are blooming torn plastic.
Combines at midnight in the standing corn,

children in black cloaks
seesawing the chained playground
(no soundtrack).

She's out there,
too like a deer to be downed,
shock of sucked milk in a baby's mouth.

The night taking names
in its notebook of stars.

WOOD SONG ⬦⬦⬦⬦⬦⬦⬦⬦⬦⬦⬦⬦⬦⬦⬦⬦

We each have our slice
of the dark
crossed or uncrossed
by the wild.

The doe puts herself
in danger, makes
less noise walking
than a cat

frights
at gust or birdcall
cupped ears
in command of the heart.

Before snow
came cloud, came
the northerly flow
of ice and hardscrabble.

The signified
is underfoot.
How hard it is
in truth

to break ground.
Will you come
to your name
will you

RAPT

Fires
are bellowed,
apples drop.

Three barebacked horses
impatient with hay
know something is dying.

Even the dolls
drooped in their tiny chairs
with uncorrupted hearts

know it
and the half-life of windows
opening onto forever

where couples whirl the margins
of a barn floor
arm-in-arm, boots beating time.

This
is your season.
You raise your hand

and watch, from far off,
your shadow
waving.

SUMMONS ◇◇◇◇◇◇◇◇◇◇◇◇◇◇◇

to Toni Flores

If you find yourself
by twilight, by seeming
accident

in a small pool
of silence
between three trees

stooped
to inhale the bruised
afterglow of roses,

I admit
I've
called you down.

Moonblind, lost,
your footsteps shimmy
the hung air,

your shawl's a scrim
of fireflies
swept out

into constellation.
Still
yourself

you would parse
the afterlife,
serve up its Elysian cocktails,

let slip that
Jupiter is bright but not
as bright as Venus,

all that and more
but for
the tamping down

of parts
that's left you
thin

as the ring
I twist in my empty hand.
Gravity

downplays us.
The whole garden
of the living

quivers.
You
turn aside—

past luck
past words
past tense.

THE LAST HORSEMAN

Those days you knew where you stood
vis-à-vis towns. There were walls.
Most of the world fell outside them.

Ravines and ditches were ours, stone
too bleak for breaking. We gave way
to roads, the morning traffic

of dukes, pigs, geese, and carts of wine.
Abundance only set the mark
to measure shortage by.

By siesta time,
the road had yellowed;
unhoused, we yellowed too.

So he did not see us,
that last horseman,
when the age of processions

was over, when the sky
smoked with weeds and manure—our
contribution—when he hung

between the town behind
and the town ahead
with his grief or last intention

moving as if toward a night's rest.

WE'LL NEVER
CHANGE OUR TUNE ◇◇◇◇◇◇◇◇◇◇◇◇◇◇◇◇

For Uzma Khan

We'd failed.
So had the world.
On the horizon
two planes tangoed to earth:
we saw them blow.

The girl with me
seemed unimpressed.
Bombers were passé.
For her, a manhole
meant the threat of a man
inside. A field of mud
might flower in worms.

So when I say we'd failed
I mean me and the planes
belting out that song called
brute force, all rhyme and reason locked
in a soundproof room,
off-key, refugeed.

Then how did she and I come
to carry such splendid swords?
She says they're just
the shined-up edges of our dreams.

23

We carry them into the dark kitchen.
She lights the stove with hers. I slice
at a vanishing cry.

(The Gulf War, 1991)

WATCH ✺✺✺✺✺✺✺✺✺✺✺✺✺✺✺✺✺

The counting of blessings
starts low to the ground.

The next day I fell ill.

All that happened
was light, no
end in sight
but itself, each day
starting over
and not from scratch.

Suck holes
under seeming ground.
A black dog
in a black shadow,
its collar jingling.

And here's Miss Premonition
wagging a bony finger,
a charter bus
gasping up the hill,
destination: *No Place Special.*

Behind, inside,
I'm ignoring the evidence,
the pale, unwritten walls,

taking as measure
the sun's queasy angle
on the morning shutter

the acceleration of cars
the assent of doves

the several tempos
of the creek, unseen.

Where you eddy
is who you are.

Each clock with its separate
count.

Take as measure
the each and every
bit whole,
unbidden.

DAYBREAK ◆◆◆◆◆◆◆◆◆◆◆◆◆◆◆◆◆

Daybreak rounds corners like a one-tuned
whistler, shoos mist from hedges, by noon
blares orders like the nanny we quaked
before: "No ma'am, I wouldn't dream of it, ma'am."
Why shouldn't we dream if we like?
Think of the donkey who day and night
brays stridently for nothing
as if nothing had to be summoned.
For the sweeter part of love is waiting.
Come wind, come weather. Let light give pause.
That blown leaf can be angel's wing or bat's.
One turn divides this world from another,
the vanishing point a chameleon's switching eye.

LANDSCAPE ◊◊◊◊◊◊◊◊◊◊◊◊◊◊◊◊◊

The eye is aimed at.
Hounds give chase in the throat.
Oh island, oh man.
The underbrush is ripping
my ankles though we kiss
and kiss. I have climbed the cliffs
where the wives wait,
quicksand and crazy currents
beneath. The children
never learned to swim.
We knit their names into mist.

Buzzards huddle.
Headlights drift the hills
remote as stars. The sun
is only a star
(you knew that) but once
upon a time we
drank it neat.
The tense is passing.
The path to your ear
is cemented, fenced.

In the suburbs of the heart is
where we live now.

BOG

(The West of Ireland)

A bold child is a punished child.

Women guard the hearth, their men
waist-deep in water holes

nick roots, unearth
pearled oak, antlers, ordinary
turf—
            rot's dark accumulation.

Muck is luck. It comes loose
as sod, runs deep
as conviction.
                It grows
by not living, by failing
to circulate.

Its mother tongue
is water.
             Nowhere to flow.

FOR THIS IS THE
FALL OF THE YEAR ◇◇◇◇◇◇◇◇◇◇◇◇◇◇◇◇

Season
of hoods,
each window touched
by a torch.

The tombstones
up all night, dancing.

    "Do you have time
    with you?" asks
    the ancient woman
    bent to an *L*

    meaning no more
    than my watch.

Color lies in state
on the leaf-slick lanes
where we fight
for something to grip.

The beloved's left-behind
cloak or cup.

If we had time
and slid through the target-
rich world like a seed

if we seeded
by day by night
runoff singing the gully...

But look at the children—
chances
thrown at life,
handfuls of stardust
streaking the dark.

No such thing
            as a line:

        "You might have starved
        while you were still
        your own ancestor"

broken up mid-
flight in the throat
of the world's wide yawn.

COTTAGE BY THE
BEACH, NORMANDY

The table's set for two, but she'll eat
alone. A dozen tulips, erect in the centerpiece,
hold their allotment of empty air.

She's old enough to have seen things that for me
are dinner-table chat: how my father
parachuted into this village, got trapped

in a farmhouse cupboard while German officers
met over lunch, waited, gun ready—went undiscovered.
Who can I thank for his life, and mine?

Not this old woman who maybe hid
beneath her bed and, embarrassed as if she'd taken
bread from a child, survived.

At her cottage by the beach where tourists tramp,
no one comes to take the second seat.
There's tea left in the pot, a clean plate to put away,

and watching from the window,
a porcelain dog, bleary-eyed, chipped,
long past welcome.

THE BALLOONS ◇◇◇◇◇◇◇◇◇◇◇◇◇◇◇◇

Those get-well balloons
dumb bottle-nosed
bubbles
weighted by ribbons and stones
or tied to baskets of fruit,
brainless, bred
for cheerful longevity—
they take over the room,
deploy the light.

They've outlived you.

Tugged free,
bobbing the ceiling
or sifting lazily down
to snag on stiff
begonias and violets,
they are circles of blustery
bravado
blurting out
their rainbowed *don't worry*,
chummy waltzers
taking a spin
in the bright squares
of picture windows.

They've outlived you,
their secret orders:
expose the rings
beneath our eyes.

Till come week three
on the sly at night
I knife them
one by one
with an ordinary
kitchen knife

let go
the quick burble of helium
the skittish collapse
of mylar, render them
tinfoil flat, crumpled,
bagged.

No more consolations.
No more
the dry eyes
of their useless god.

34

WHEREOF ARE YOU MADE ◇◇◇◇◇◇

What is your substance, whereof are you made
that millions of strange shadows on you tend…
—Shakespeare

As if you made me
to find you, after
(thumbing pictures at my desk)
to follow back
your orphaned trail
through Ellis Island
to the Cyrillic scribblings
on back of stagy
nineteenth-century photos
to where your name is rescued
from simplifications,
to where, I can't be sure,
I might find the single uncle
surviving with a limp,
all the others burned out or gassed,
and here's you at eight
at a Coney Island booth
with a stare that assumes
the future.

Abandoned, silenced,
what did you win—
me to tell this?

◇◇◇

You helped a rocket
take a close-up of the moon,
stroked the sky with radar.
How often together we
looked up into the space
you could photograph, listen in
on, but never inhabit

like the darkness inside houses
where faith dwindles
to a string,
light losing its grip on objects,
sofa and chair
vague as good intentions,
the leftover crenelations of a man's dream.

◇◇◇

Six weeks gone, you
worry about the weather
about my getting home safe
in the blubbering snow—
"How are you managing, kid?"
I willingly recite the week's
bland details to the windshield
driving through the shaken
quilt of dusk, shocked
to be chatting so casually
with the dead.

◇◇◇

But you were always
away
skimming continents,
even home, didn't come
to the phone,
let mom relay the news

so six weeks dead
it's not farfetched to think
you'll suddenly call
from some airport,
take a connecting flight,
visit.

◆◆◆

The wearing away of cloth
into lint,
flies swarming the bloated belly
of the roadside deer,
the trees weeping sugar.
So much finds its way
back, regardless
of the missing landmarks,
the thin wire vibrating old news.

◆◆◆

Clouds drop shadows
on the scrubbed lake,
bare trees inscribe it.

If I could follow their design
it might lead to trunk
and root, the earth itself
where you
are held and whole
till imagination collapses,
the sides of the box fall in.

◆◆◆

Forsythia yellow
dulls to green.
Lilacs unfist themselves.

Six weeks gone, your watch
under the armchair,
flung by medics,
still ticking.

In memory of my father

CHILDREN'S
BEACH MUSEUM ◇◇◇◇◇◇◇◇◇◇◇◇◇◇◇◇

Just beyond the beach
where sea turtles
lay their eggs by moonlight
this time of year

a few maimed specimens
are kept for children
to look at—one baby
loggerhead, its left front leg

a jellied fin, another
flowering papillomas,
ocean water pumping
through a buried pipe.

They surface and stare,
bald heads fixed,
would snap a baby's fist off
gladly.

Inside, under glass, stuffed
snappers and box turtles poise,
and this owl, removed from a wire,
one leg burned off, feathers on end.

Grimly my daughter
surveys their fates,
glares speechless at the cheerful
volunteer guide, retracing the steps

she took just last month
with her patient grandfather,
his death still hidden in him
like her fist tight in a pocket.

THE MIRACULOUS
MANDARIN

They knew how your good looks
would bring men
off the street,
how a cave is a good place
to invisibly linger—
no, not you,
you were to be out front,
the three brothers inside
waiting for wealthy victims,
waiting tense as spiders.
They promised you a cut.
And we must remember that all this
takes place in a poor country.
Well, you brought them in
all right, first a bankrupt cavalier
then a thin student, but
they weren't worth the air they
breathed—the brothers threw them out
their copper bits flung after them
and said move fast and quiet
if you know what's good for you,
and they did.

Then the mandarin came along,
a traveling collector with silk-lined

pockets and an oiled moustache.
He is called miraculous,
but how much of a miracle
was it, really, that he fell for you
on the spot—you *were* alluring—
that he rose to your dance,
his face a sad dog's,
and when the men pounced,
found gold, then tried
to smother him with his own silk sack,
his eyes, fixed to yours,
kept him alive, ready,
so that even when their knife
ripped open his guts,
he still breathed
and had to have you
though the murderers shrieked
"Die, die!" he could
not, lurching
like a haywire top,
a danse macabre that would not finish,
his eyes still on you, so
that was the miracle then:
that desire could keep the heart
beating against all odds...
but that's no revelation, is it,
nor that when
you gave yourself to him
right there in front of
the embarrassed schemers,
when you shimmied along his blood

and kissed his eyes shut
that only then could he die
for you, and did.

MYRRHA ◆◆◆◆◆◆◆◆◆◆◆◆◆◆◆◆◆◆

*(After Ovid: Myrrha, having slept with her father and
conceived a son, Adonis, is changed into the myrrh tree.)*

A new tree wasn't worth so great a price.
No boy in sight was your match,
though often you'd fall half in treacherous love,
seeking yourself in one
as if you'd been misplaced.

And father was no mere father
but Aphrodite's fawn, love's
well-loved priest,
twin-gifted with song and lust.
You could aim no higher.
                                        Only

because you are his, you may not be his.
Three times you stumbled in the darkened hall.
Three times the screech owl uncannily
cried out. But you, unrecognized,
found yourself in his bed.

Mother-to-be of a brother,
sister to a son, you begged relief
and even as you prayed
your toes thinned out to roots,
your bones gained strength

and the earth shut over your legs.
So the boy Adonis,
slipped from your split trunk,
came out gleaming with that scent
he could never rub himself free of—

myrrh, carried forward,
millennium to millennium,
as a gift.

GROUNDED ◆◆◆◆◆◆◆◆◆◆◆◆◆◆◆◆◆

The staccato slap
of a door
my only answer.

I opened a book
I wasn't reading,
the radio in its secret drawer

chirped *verboten* dreams,
a bee whirling
in the hive of my heart.

I was the stuff of honey,
the flower flattened
by rain. My name was mangled.

See the doorway
edged in light? I proved light
by shadows.

I spelled myself.
Love, like a library book,
changed hands.

NIGHT REPAIR CREAM ⬦⬦⬦⬦⬦⬦⬦⬦⬦⬦⬦⬦⬦⬦⬦

When I called the price of the cream she'd talked me into
outlandish, the saleswoman crooned,
"That's an investment in the future
of you."

The me-to-be, to be
like her?—falling cheeks
propped up with rouge,
hair gelled to tidiness.

(Oh the smooth cheek of girlhood,
my daughter's black braid
quivering over a perfect back—
only to become a buyer of lotions?)

My face (I see it now) a solemn elder I'd once
have craved advice from,
eons from the girl lost in Chopin,
the woman lost among kimonos, unfolding. . . .

What would I pay for *that* face?
All right, she's already
rung it up,
packed it in a tiny golden bag.

The store air pulses with opening flowers.
"Enjoy," she calls after,
adjusting the mirrors,
pricing the hours till night.

HEAT ◊◊◊◊◊◊◊◊◊◊◊◊◊◊◊◊

Longing's lightning strike
and the savory simmer
after. You
is all and all
is else. Footfall,
stride, the fields

slipping to water
where an old woman stares
from summer whites,
head cocked
to the hum of what passes,
its vanishing backside.

The farther we walk
out where the river decides
which crop, which ditch,
the daisies blurring to haze,
the memorized shoreline,
the sinking dock. . . .

Our lingo is *want*,
its little star-shaped flare
worn as a necklace
inflected over verge,

over *if* and *as*
(the ways he has).

The last lit window's
paling, the wrinkled parchment
of soil, the evening wind
chiseling away
at the polished edge
of what we will not speak.

MARCHING ORDERS

Fool, foot in the grave,
as if hemlock were heroic,
as if age were tremulous
in a bay of stars.
Darkling, we creature.
The features of fear
are hammered, human,
the mote in the mind
your truest neighbor.
It outleaps pardon.

Too many hours I lay
at his feet. Be dis-
enthralled, annealed.
The well-wrought
winged thing in the heart,
the leeward isles,
back-lit—old tunes
to turn your head.

BOUQUET ·······················

Some kinds of courage are orchids,
others daisies. "I'm tired of a life
that deepens as it dries in place,"
you say, and stomp off through the field.

Our bickering breath,
gathered on the window, has cast
a delicate bouquet through which
I watch you pace the near horizon.

Look, our house is airy, plain,
temple to small companion things
you kick at as clutter, coming in,
head field-dizzy, with your offer—

a handful of wildflowers.

WINTER FIELD ◇◇◇◇◇◇◇◇◇◇◇◇◇◇◇◇◇

Mornings the lake makes itself a cloud out of
pure cold and water. We can only watch.
Perhaps we're here, like cows, so we can give,
I say, though I remember how we laughed
about that bishop who thought animals
were only in the world to keep meat fresh.
We wondered where that might leave us. "Winter
under cultivation is as arable
as Spring," says Dickinson. So we walk
the January fields, breathing a blizzard
of dry seeds, ploughing our way through stubble.
At dusk new snow rubs out our traces. I
open my mouth to the sky till I know
my place, my center, this: where you plant your kiss.

ANTENATAL ◆◆◆◆◆◆◆◆◆◆◆◆◆◆◆◆

You'll want to know from where you've come. Should
I say: that Friday the shadow of a crow
crossed my hand, the house huddled in its clump
of landscape, cold held the buds in ransom...
Or should I tell how weeks later I first saw you
on a screen, swaddled in what looked like a tear
(though no tears have yet come between us)
your confident heart mine in unerring
double time, your head already astir
in thoughts and music—what I mean to give,
what I can't filter out. This summer
face-down in water, we swim back and forth
together, shadows flawlessly attune,
forgetting that you'll ever break into the light.

TOUCHED

At the ballet,
a woman sits down beside me,
sticks her hands on my pregnant belly, says
"How are *we* tonight?"

Her embarrassed teenage daughter slumps
into the next seat
while you let loose
with a few good thumps.

I don't know why I tell you this—
you seemed to enjoy the music at least
and you'll soon meet many faces like that woman's
coming at you uninvited.

But I want you to know
how sad it made me—
this first time you were touched by someone
who wasn't going to love you.

CLEANING SMELT

Snipped at the neck:
tangerine roe, milky innards,
their mouths jerked open
for a final sentence.

One bowl for guts and eyes,
one for their stiff,
edible bodies.
The baby inside me bolts.

"Off with their heads,
off with their heads,"
my three-year-old
marches the kitchen

keen for dinner.
She pauses only
for a vase of wilted
daffodils, dying,

she proclaims,
like the dinosaurs,
like clothes that get too small
while you're wearing them.

PRAYER ◇◇◇◇◇◇◇◇◇◇◇◇◇◇◇◇◇

The Deer Crossing signs are riddled with bullets,
practiced on pre-season,
and now heads of deer
tilt from car roofs, distracted.
We are their only predators.
This is our season.

The stars fatten like pearls.
Not enough light to read your face by.
And useless to wish on, as restless
as we are, growing or shrinking.
All we can do
is lend our bodies to life.

Listen, in the tall bushes, a bird crying out
in a voice so like a grieving woman's
it wrenches apples from the trees.
Dear mother-of-pearl, firmament
in which we graze, scatter your milk.
It's so hard to feed at God's body.

WINTER SOLSTICE

1.

A black nasturtium
in a glass bowl, water
genuflecting
to the vibration of buses,
footsteps—ours,
the neighbors' bearing
gifts of the season
and cups to borrow sugar.

Firewood drops into ash.
A child's laughter
drops into doubt.
An island of flower
registers the shrinking day.

2.

Can you streak it
like a comet, sidle up
to the circling hawk,
be bat haunting
hat brims,
cousin to enormity,
innocent of shadow?

3.

No one's
home. The restless perfume
of a peony
empties from a painted lute.

Observation claims
the garden will outlast the house
the house the woman
bulbed into black blossom.

The log outlasts
the tree, the fire
its hissing.

4.

we do not know how to cry
our mothers say that death is instant
will the thought of us ever hurt you
we have already forgotten our fathers
please bury us in the River Una
the nicest river in the world
and the only being who can leave Bihac

5.

A hillside of markers,
a showroom of tombs.
The bushes fruited with ice.

FINAL ELSEWHERE

In memoriam, Joseph Brodsky

First you must
take off your jacket,
the civilizing tie,

must tightrope
cross the sky
on a bridge of zeroes,

see can you
stanch
the outpour,

pocket magma,
glean magnetic north.
But first

you must take off
your glasses, turn in
your books and cigarettes

confess to zeroes
in headlights
and laurel wreaths,

the zero of the sun,
even
your belated wedding ring.

The heart
is an island
momentarily bridged.

The cemetery angels
welcome you
without blinking an eye.

COMMITMENT ◆◆◆◆◆◆◆◆◆◆◆◆◆◆◆◆◆

If we say *this is your home now*
it means we're leaving

the windows
wincing shut

a walleyed woman
to fill your daily orders

though behind her
a sign instructs

eat less
of the food the living need.

Blossoms leap
into the spongy grass

a field comes to graze
at an open grave

your only mirror:
my hurt gaze.

THE RULE OF BERRIES

The honey-feast of the berries has stunned them;
they believe in heaven.

—Sylvia Plath

The stream sided with berries
(pick them for the clabbered cream)
running with berry juice, stream juice
and the quick eyes of blackbirds
—I am tilted
perilous off the bank,
hand threading branches,
my old blood sister holding hard
the other hand for ballast,
bush after bush, water-
and light-fed, till
pail full, the stream
passing into bog, its other work,
we go home to the rule
of berries—jam, cobbler, pie. Remember?
Rosemary roasting on the lamb that night,
what it meant to be together there
far out over the stream as we dared lean
trusting the other's hand
years after we'd grown cautious,
separate—
to hear it still: spill
of berries in the bucket, girlish shrieks
of wet feet, our hands
lovely and stained again.

for Wendy Shankin Cohen

63

BAPTISMAL ◇◇◇◇◇◇◇◇◇◇◇◇◇◇◇◇◇◇

for Katherine Penn Scully

You're meant to believe in fertile country:
olive greens and ochres
wall your nursery
and your mother's peach face and breasts
are summer fruits you're fed year-round.

We're busy talking
when you look away to the window
you don't know as glass yet,
a scene framed white
like a picture postcard of another country

taped up as souvenir.
There, a row of leafless poplars
is all that keeps you from grey hills
and a sky gone blank
with twilight

where human evening now
aims its amber lights
and the stars take their place behind
the pulsing reds of the army airfield
where night marches in ways we cannot imagine.

Imagine, Katherine.

GESTURE ◇◇◇◇◇◇◇◇◇◇◇◇◇◇◇◇◇

Set to force the dying doe
into deep water, we wade out
till my father stumbles—

he raised her since a fawn,
holds back my hand. Stunned
in place, water rising,

we look to the sky
to find ourselves
single-minded, cleared,

but like wasps who
batter themselves on window glass
ignoring open air behind,

as hard as we look
we see ourselves still
as we are,

there, chilled,
doubt obvious as blood on snow,
as the raven waiting,

until the doe between us
cradles the crown of her head
in seawater, rocks her hurt

into tide, stirs
the dormant night plankton
into a trail of greenish stars.

ETERNITY IN DAYS ◆◆◆◆◆◆◆◆◆◆◆◆◆◆

One last lick of daylight
lids the lake. Smoke
thins,

rising. What's
freedom for?
If you could

you'd open like a door,
declare *forever*
in the winding stream

that empties
at your feet.
If not for

weather
you would piece the sky,
stitch

the day-to-day,
the dotted lines of property,
unto the lapped horizon.

What's freedom
for? *Will Divide,*
Will Build to Suit—

whole hillsides shorn,
every creature in earshot,
in living memory,

plumbing
the dark, unmarked
waters.

CONSTELLATED ⬦⬦⬦⬦⬦⬦⬦⬦⬦⬦⬦⬦⬦⬦

for David

Head to foot in a firmament
of blankets, our bellies bursting stars,
7 degrees northwest of Mira the Wonderful
in the heart of Pisces I've found us: that
double star, Al-Rescha, that ties the knot
of the fishes' tails, seen as one
by the naked eye, but in truth a 700-year-long
do-si-do. Love owes its safety
to our patience. Or call it gravity,
what keeps us dancing
in our wobbly orbit, pale green and blue
in the home of loaves and fishes.
My shimmery one, my principle
of attraction, dreamers
wish on us. We are the cord that binds,
self-luminous. We cannot be blown
off course, we cannot be
blown out.

Notes

"Remains"
   "The butterfly preaches contentment" —Rudyard Kipling
   "We are as water…" —II Samuel 14:14

"Spirit"
   "Go and catch a falling star…" —Donne

"Bog"
   My thanks to Phillip Snyder for generously sharing his
   research on bogs

"For This Is the Fall of the Year"
   "You might have starved while you were still your own
   ancestor" —John Ciardi in an NPR broadcast

"Winter Solstice"
   "We do not know how to cry…" —an e-mail received in
   Ithaca, New York, from children in Bihac during the
   Bosnian War

"Final Elsewhere"
   The phrase "final elsewhere" is from Susan Sontag's
   afterword to Mikhail Lemkhin's *Joseph Brodsky Leningrad*

"Eternity in Days"
   The title and the phrase "What's freedom for?" echo the
   last stanza of Theodore Roethke's "I Knew a Woman"

The Author

DEBORAH TALL is the author of three
previous books of poems (most
recently *Come Wind, Come Weather*
from State Street Press) and two
books of nonfiction: *The Island of the
White Cow: Memories of an Irish Island*
(Atheneum, 1986) and *From Where We
Stand: Recovering a Sense of Place* (Knopf,
1993; paperback, Johns Hopkins

Neil Sjoblem

University Press, 1996). Tall edits the poetry journal *Seneca
Review* and is co-editor of the anthology *The Poet's Notebook*
(Norton, 1995). She has taught writing and literature at
Hobart and William Smith Colleges since 1982 and lives in
Ithaca, New York, with her husband, poet David Weiss, and
their two daughters.